OUT OF THE LAB
EXTREME JOBS IN SCIENCE

PALEONTOLOGISTS AND ARCHAEOLOGISTS

by Ruth Owen

PowerKiDS
press

New York

Published in 2014 by The Rosen Publishing Group, Inc.
29 East 21st Street, New York, NY 10010

First Edition

Produced for Rosen by Ruby Tuesday Books Ltd
Editor for Ruby Tuesday Books Ltd: Mark J. Sachner
US Editor: Joshua Shadowens
Designer: Tammy West and Emma Randall

Photo Credits:
Cover, 5, 7, 8, 19 © Superstock; 1, 6, 12–13, 16–17, 18, 20–21, 23 (top), 28–29 © Shutterstock; 9, 15 © Science Photo Library; 11 © Getty Images; 14 © NASA; 21 (top) © Wikipedia Creative Commons; 22–23 © Ricardo Liberato; 25 © AERA Inc; 26–27 © Alamy.

Publisher Cataloging Data

Owen, Ruth.
Paleontologists and archaeologists / by Ruth Owen. — First edition.
   p. cm. — (Out of the lab: extreme jobs in science)
Includes index.
ISBN 978-1-4777-1290-0 (library binding) — ISBN 978-1-4777-1380-8 (pbk.) — ISBN 978-1-4777-1387-7 (6-pack)
1. Archaeologists — Juvenile literature. 2. Paleontologists — Juvenile literature. 3. Archaeology — Juvenile literature. 4. Paleontology — Juvenile literature. I. Owen, Ruth, 1967–. II. Title.
QE714.7 O94 2014
560.92—dc23

Manufactured in the United States of America

CPSIA Compliance Information: Batch #S13PK8: For Further Information contact Rosen Publishing, New York, New York at 1-800-237-9932

Contents

A DISCOVERY IN THE DESERT

Slowly and very carefully, the excited group of scientists chipped away at a large piece of rock buried in the scorching sand.

Using soft brushes and small ice-pick-like tools called **awls**, they removed rock and sand from around a huge **fossil.** Ignoring the burning desert heat, they continued to work until finally they had revealed an enormous fossilized skull.

It was 1997, and the scientists were in the Sahara Desert, in Africa. They were there to look for dinosaurs, but what they'd found was a giant, prehistoric crocodile with a head as long as an adult human! **Paleontologist** and **expedition** leader Paul Sereno, realized they had found a **specimen** of *Sarcosuchus imperator*, a massive creature that lived 110 million years ago.

SCIENCE IN ACTION

Paul Sereno's desert expedition site was in an area where winds can blow at 80 miles per hour (130 km/h) causing blinding sandstorms. It was difficult to know how hot it was because the temperature rose higher than a normal thermometer, which goes up to 120°F (49°C), could measure!

A scientist sits beside a life-size
model of *Sarcosuchus imperator*.

WHAT IS A PALEONTOLOGIST?

A paleontologist is a scientist who studies the history of living things by examining fossils.

Paleontologists study the fossils of large animals such as dinosaurs, small animals such as insects, plants, **fungi**, and even microscopic **bacteria**. The fossilized remains of an animal can be used to understand how it moved, what it ate, how it reproduced, and many other facts about its behavior and everyday life. Before a fossil can be studied, however, it has to be found!

Fossils form in rock so paleontologists break open rocks to look inside them. They also carefully examine cliffs, mountain slopes, or areas of stony ground hoping to spot a small part of a fossil jutting out from a rock.

A fossilized plant ➤

How do fossils form? When an ancient animal dies, layers of **sediment**, such as sand, cover its skeleton. In time, the animal's bones crumble away and the sediment fills the spaces left by the bones. More layers of sediment then settle above and press together to form rock. After millions of years, fossils, or rock copies, of the animal's bones form.

A paleontologist uncovers a *Sarcosuchus* fossil in the desert.

An awl

7

EXCAVATING FOSSILS

Once a fossil has been discovered, it has to be carefully removed from the rock surrounding it.

If the fossil is in a hot desert or on a steep rocky cliff, it means the paleontologist **excavating** the fossil must work in uncomfortable or sometimes dangerous conditions. To chip away the rock around a fossil, paleontologists use small hammers, awls, and sometimes dental instruments. Everyday tools such as paintbrushes and toothbrushes are used to brush away dust and fragments of rock.

A *Sarcosuchus* fossil

Once the fossil is revealed, it has to be protected. It is covered in glue or wrapped in plaster, the kind that's used to fix a broken arm or leg. Then the fossil is taken to a **laboratory** to be cleaned and studied.

SCIENCE IN ACTION

As paleontologists work, they record everything they do by keeping notes, taking photographs, and making videos.

A place where fossils are being excavated is often called "a dig." Here, a team of paleontologists are carefully removing fossils from rock at a dig. ▼

SUPERCROC REVEALED

After the discovery of the giant crocodile skull in the Sahara Desert, paleontologist Paul Sereno and his team eventually unearthed about 50 percent of the monster crocodile's skeleton.

The paleontologists had found enough of the creature they nicknamed SuperCroc to figure out that the massive beast weighed around 20,000 pounds (9,000 kg) and was 40 feet (12 m) long. Its jaws contained 100 teeth and were powerful enough to catch and crush not only fish and turtles but small dinosaurs, too.

During expeditions to the Sahara Desert, Paul Sereno has also discovered fossils of a plant-eating dinosaur called *Nigersaurus* and a huge meat-eater called *Carcharodontosaurus*.

SCIENCE IN ACTION

Paul's 1997 expedition to the Sahara Desert involved transporting people, tents, tools, and enough supplies for the team for four months. The supplies included 4,000 gallons (15,000 l) of water and 600 pounds (270 kg) of pasta!

Paul Sereno

Carcharodontosaurus skull

POLAR BEARS AND SAUSAGES

When people think of a paleontologist searching for dinosaur fossils, they usually imagine a person working in a hot, dusty environment. Some **paleontology** expeditions take place in very cold places, though.

Dr. Pat Druckenmiller is a paleontologist who specializes in studying dinosaurs that lived in the ocean. Pat carries out his fossil hunting in Alaska.

When Pat goes on an expedition, he might find himself riding a boat on an icy Alaskan **fjord** to get to the area he wants to investigate. Once he's pitched his tent, he has to set trip wires to protect the camp from polar bears. If a bear touches one of the wires, it sets off a flare that explodes and hopefully scares the animal away!

SCIENCE IN ACTION

During an expedition in the cold Alaskan environment, Pat eats lots of fatty foods, such as sausages. In extreme cold, a person's body burns up energy fast keeping warm. So Pat's super-fatty diet gives his body the fuel it needs to survive the extreme conditions.

Home for a paleontologist is often a tent for weeks or months at a time.

Paleontology can be dangerous if you're on an expedition in an area that's home to 1,200 pound (500 kg) meat-eaters!

THE SEARCH FOR ANCIENT HUMANS

Not all paleontologists dig for ancient dinosaurs. Louise Leakey searches for fossils of ancient humans at Lake Turkana, in the Rift Valley, in East Africa.

Louise's parents are paleontologists, so was her grandfather. In fact, Louise was taken on her first research expedition when she was just six weeks old!

The Rift Valley is a vast basin in the land. Rivers flow down into the valley from highland areas carrying sediment. Over millions of years, the sediment has covered and preserved the bones of the animals and early humans that once made the valley their home. Today, Louise, her mother, Meave Leakey, and teams of fossil hunters work on the shores of Lake Turkana searching for ancient human remains.

river

river

This is a satellite image of Lake Turkana. The lake is nearly 250 miles (400 km) long, so the area to search for fossils is enormous.

In 1984, when Louise was 12 years old, her father Richard Leakey and his team of fossil hunters discovered a fossilized skeleton of the ancient human species *Homo erectus*. The skeleton was a boy who'd died when he was around 12 years old.

The discovery of Turkana Boy (his skull is seen here) was an exciting time for young Louise Leakey and helped her to decide that she would be a paleontologist.

FINDING FRAGMENTS

Searching for ancient human remains at Lake Turkana is not easy!

Fossil hunters slowly walk across vast stretches of rocky ground. It's tiring, time-consuming work, but they can not lose their concentration. Lying among stones and grit could be a tiny fossil that unlocks an important part of the human story. The only clue to the location of the Turkana Boy skeleton was a fragment of skull on the ground that was smaller than a playing card!

When Louise and her team find a fossil, before moving it they take photographs and use **GPS** to pinpoint and record its location. Knowing exactly where a fossil was found can help piece together an ancient animal or human's story if more fossils are later found nearby.

SCIENCE IN ACTION

In 2001, Louise and her mother discovered a new species of human, named *Kenyanthropus platyops*. This species lived 3.5 million years ago. The story of our human history is a long timeline with many mysteries still to be solved. This is what makes Louise's work so exciting!

You're hot, hungry, tired, and you've been searching for fossils for hours. Would you spot the fragment of *Homo erectus* jawbone among the rocks and stones here?

WHAT IS AN ARCHAEOLOGIST?

An **archaeologist** is a scientist who learns about the past by finding and then examining objects or ancient sites, such as burial grounds or the remains of buildings.

Usually the places or objects that archaeologists study have been buried underground for hundreds or thousands of years. An archaeologist might specialize in studying one period in history, a particular civilization, such as the ancient Egyptians, or a type of place, for example, **Civil War** battlefields. Some archaeologists specialize in studying particular types of **artifacts**, such as coins, pottery, or weapons.

Like paleontologists, archaeologists spend part of their time working outside at archaeological digs. They also spend time in laboratories analyzing the things they find.

Just a piece of stone in some mud? No! It's a Stone Age tool that's over 5,000 years old!

▲ At a dig, archaeologists excavate items by carefully removing the layers of soil that have built up on top of them. They use tools such as small trowels and brushes.

UNDERWATER ARCHAEOLOGY

Most artifacts and ancient buildings are buried underground on land. Some, however, are buried under sediment beneath the ocean, or the waters of lakes.

An underwater dig may begin with a boat ride to the dig's location. Then it's into the water wearing scuba diving gear.

Archaeologists often create a rope grid over a dig site. This acts like the lines on a map allowing particular places or finds to be pinpointed on the grid map. Underwater archaeologists do this, too. The team members hammer iron bars, or posts, into the sea or lakebed. Then they attach long ropes in a criss-cross pattern to the bars. Everything found in the grid is noted on the scientists' dive slates, photographed, and recorded on video.

SCIENCE IN ACTION

Because they need to be working on the seabed, underwater archaeologists wear heavy, weighted belts. The belts stop them from floating up or moving around too much as they concentrate on their work.

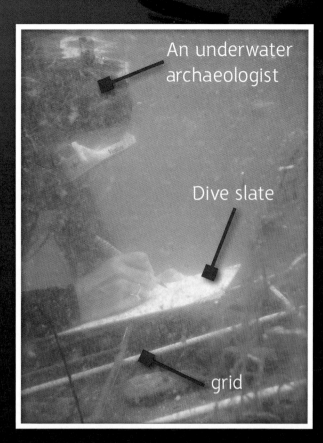

An underwater archaeologist

Dive slate

grid

Artifacts on the seabed at a dig site

BONE COLLECTING

On any given day, archaeologist Richard Redding might be surrounded by cattle skulls, the leg bones of sheep, and many other animal bones.

To some it might seem gruesome, but Richard's bone-collecting activities in Egypt are helping to uncover secrets about the lives of the ancient Egyptian workers who built the pyramids.

Along with a team of archaeologists, Richard has excavated and identified over 175,000 bones from a workers' village at the Pyramids of Giza. The collection includes bones from cattle, sheep, and goats.

The Pyramids at Giza, in Egypt ▲

It was once believed that the pyramid builders were poorly treated slaves. Now archaeological evidence seems to show that the pyramid builders were well fed on fresh meat. This suggests they were valued workers with a good quality of life.

A sheep's skull

Richard Redding analyzes animal bones from archaeological sites to find out information such as what people ate or how they produced their food. He is known as an archaeozoologist.

LIFE IN THE WORKERS' VILLAGE

The bones found in the workers' village close to the pyramids are around 4,500 years old.

The large numbers of bones found shows that around 4,000 pounds (1,800 kg) of meat was produced every day to feed the thousands of construction workers. In addition to meat, the workers were fed fish, lentils, beans, grains, and beer.

To graze enough animals to fulfill the meat requirements of the workers' village would take an area the size of Los Angeles. So archaeologists believe the animals were raised by farmers throughout the region, then brought to the worker's village to be **slaughtered**. This is similar to the way that modern-day farmers raise animals then take them to a meat-processing plant to be slaughtered and sold.

SCIENCE IN ACTION

Archaeologists can use the remains and artifacts they find to create pictures or models that show how ancient places might have looked.

This artwork shows how the pyramid builders' accommodation might have looked.

Named the corral, archaeologists believe this area at the workers' village is an enclosure where animals were kept before they were slaughtered.

BONE COLLECTING: BEHIND THE SCENES

To identify an animal bone, Richard Redding must have a previously identified skeleton he can compare it to. So Richard tries to collect skeletons from as many different animals as possible.

When Richard finds or is given an animal carcass for his collection, he gets to work cutting off as much flesh as possible. This can be smelly work, especially in the heat of a country such as Egypt. What's left of the carcass then goes into Richard's "bug box." Inside this large plastic box is a colony of **scavenging** beetles. The larvae, or young, of the beetles feed on decaying flesh. The insects strip every morsel of flesh from the bones, leaving Richard a perfectly clean skeleton for his bone collection.

SCIENCE IN ACTION

So many amazing artifacts have been found in Egypt, but Richard Redding's simple sheep and cattle bones have been able to tell an important story about how the pyramid builders lived and how they were treated by the pharaohs for whom they worked.

Beetle larvae are eating the flesh from this gorilla skeleton.

Beetles

LIFE IN THE FIELD

Both paleontologists and archaeologists spend time in laboratories and offices, but they also spend time out of the lab working in the field.

Working at a dig can be back-breaking, though. You could be crouched in a small hole in the ground for days carefully chipping away at a piece of rock. You might be working in scorching sand or in freezing cold mud. A large dinosaur skeleton or ancient building can take months of patient work to uncover. During that time you might be living in a tent in the middle of nowhere!

On the upside, a career as an archaeologist or paleontologist may give you the chance to travel the globe, work with scientists from other countries, and discover something no one else has ever seen!

SCIENCE IN ACTION

As an archaeologist or paleontologist, you can never lose patience and rush an excavation. You could destroy a piece of history that might change our understanding of the past!

Archaeologists and student volunteers work at an archaeological dig in Great Britain at the ancient Roman fort and settlement called Vindolanda.

GLOSSARY

archaeologist
(ahr-kee-AH-luh-jist) A scientist who studies the past by examining the physical remains left behind, for example buildings, skeletons, and artifacts such as coins and pottery.

artifacts (AR-tih-fakts) Objects made by humans such as coins, pottery, tools, or weapons.

awls (OLZ) A sharp, pointed tool used to aid in digs.

bacteria (bak-TIHR-ee-uh) Microscopic living things. Some bacteria are helpful, while others can cause disease.

Civil War (SIH-vul WOR) The war fought between the Northern and the Southern states of America from 1861 to 1865.

excavating
(ek-skuh-VAY-ting) Digging out something from soil or rock.

expedition (ek-spuh-DIH-shun) A group of people making a journey to a particular place to explore or investigate that place.

fjord (fee-YORD) A long, narrow waterway between high cliffs.

fossil (FO-sul) An imprint of an animal or plant's remains that has formed in rock over millions of years.

fungi (FUN-jy) A group of living things that are not plants or animals. Mushrooms and mold are types of fungi.

GPS (jee-pee-es) Stands for Global Positioning System, which is a device that helps find your location on a map.

laboratory (LA-bruh-tor-ee) A room in which scientists do tests.

paleontologist
(pay-lee-on-TO-luh-jist) A scientist who studies animals, plants, and other living things from the past by examining fossils.

paleontology
(pay-lee-on-tuh-LO-jee) The scientific study of living things from the past, primarily through the study of fossils.

scavenging (SKA-venj-ing) Feeding on dead animals or on garbage.

sediment (SEH-deh-ment) Tiny pieces of rock that have been worn away from bigger rocks by forces such as waves or wind.

slaughtered (SLAH-terd) Killed for food.

specimen (SPES-men) A sample of something or an item to be scientifically studied.

WEBSITES

Due to the changing nature of Internet links, PowerKids Press has developed an online list of websites related to the subject of this book. This site is updated regularly. Please use this link to access the list:

www.powerkidslinks.com/olejs/paleo/

READ MORE

Francis, Ian. *Dinosaur Fossils*. Real Life Readers. New York: Rosen Classroom, 2008.

Peterson, Judy Monroe. *Fossil Finders: Paleontologists*. Extreme Scientists. New York: PowerKids Press, 2008.

Spilsbury, Richard, and Louise Spilsbury. *Fossils*. Let's Rock. Mankato, MN: Heinemann, 2011.

INDEX